Unfolding Gifts In The Spirit Of Poetry

By

Di Hall

Published by Di Hall

Text Copyright © Di Hall 2016

Cover design by © Elizabeth Fitt

All rights reserved. No part of this publication may be reproduced, stored in a retrieval system, or transmitted in any form or by any means, electronic, mechanical, photocopy, recording or otherwise, without prior written permission of the copyright owner. Nor can it be circulated in any form of binding or cover other than that in which it is published and without similar condition including this condition being imposed on a subsequent purchaser.

British Library Cataloguing Publication Data.
A catalogue record for this book is available from the British Library

ISBN 978-0-9954728-1-5

Contents

In a Passage of Time

Mother of Woes 3
My Child 5
A Father in Time 7
Depression 8
Images and Dreams 10
The Tomb 12
Remembering 13
My Lost Merry Maker 15
Opposites 16
Second Birth 17
Walking with Thee 18
Finality 20

And Others

Lost Self 25
Alice's Journey 26
The Dancer 27
To Francis 28
Ambersham Green 30

Acceptance 31
More than Me 32
Orphaned 34

Sold for a Song

Christchurch Cathedral 39
Bound 40
Hells Henchmen 41
From a Sonnet to a Shepherd 42
Micro Chipped Sally (TI) 44
Emancipated 47
Escape 49
Betrayal 51
No One There 53
Revelation 55
Siren City 57
Grace and Heeding 58
Masquerading Gods 59
Suppression 61
The Scream 62

Separation, Loss & Yearning

Farewells 67
Goodbye 68
No Time to Say Goodbye 70
Grieving 72
Leaving 74
Loss 75

Loves Illusion

Love and Marriage 79
Merging 80
My Secret Love 81
Passing Love 83
Sweet Refreshing 84
Twinned Longing 85
Theatre of Dreams 86

Natures Naked Beauty

Time 91
Teacher 92
The Rock 93
Changes 94
Joy 95
Centre Ground 96
Thirsting 97
Sea Home 98
Willow Willowing 99
Untouched 100

No Place

Rhapsody 105
Jericho 106
Running 107
Systems 108
The Caldron 109
The Computerised End 110

In a Passage of Time

Mother of Woes

I held her in a world woe
and followed her down to the brook to show,
orphans, pilgrim and leopards alike.
A world away from one in fight.

I met with her eye, a sad grey stare
and reached out to the depth of her soul laid bare.
I watched the tear as if formed in her eye
then embraced her compassion for the years gone by.

Her lucent thin skin and hollow drawn look,
drew me to the storm of her life's open book.
Selfless strives of sufferings,
perilous pain, grace, faith and healing.

She taught me to love from a cleft in her heart
and engrafted mercy from a universe apart.
She gave birth to a sunflower from a button undone,
then offered me up to the true holy one.

We danced to capture a season insight
and shared in the purpose of Gods own delight.
We gave up all that grounds to sand,
then invested out time to the hope of our land.

My Child

Peel the strands that separate still
and follow me down sweet child to hear.
Cherished, beloved and begotten,
treasured, tendered babe in arms.

Playful, joyous, kindred being,
skipped in colour mingled joining.
Birthed into this holding space,
a tapestry of echoes, face to face.

Callous, cold crystal shades, so clear,
polluted pink draped in grey.
Tumble down this grass so green
and eclipse into this lifeless dream.

So innocent descent into dawning,
a garden of delight and petals falling.
Nurtured nature, transparent truth,
I bid you come to me in proof.

Urchin bathed in blueness bonding,
pearl so pale, hung in yearning.
Come creep and slip your presence near,
come cry with me, free from fear.

I will carry you on my shoulders bare
and together our stories we will share.
To run with you this journeys race,
through to eternity's kingdom love embraced.

A Father in Time

I held the tears and all the fears.
Your poverty, fame, I felt that pain.
The poison you fed to my flesh that bled.
Your mocking of love for the heavens above.

Oh, nurturer of time tempered in glory,
have mercy on this old mans story.
Of a bitter flesh in strife and plight
a spiritless being blind of insight.

The twisted nature, the thoughtless tongue,
that ends a sons life before its begun.
A battered, bruised reed destined afar,
the crippled crushed reign of this fallen star.

Depression

I walked through the time of an ageless void,
polluted in madness, experienced in full.
No chime to the hour to depict the bells;
no need of pacing or counting what fell.

Dropping perfume on rose petal buds,
salting the tears that fall from their eyes.
Shrinking, sinking, engulfed in mud,
and lost forever in its bed of lies.

Defying the Gods, a destiny imposed,
painting the lining from a position they chose.
Drawing the smoke from cinders that burned,
the sweetening of words from those that churned.

Papering the skies your smiles so wide,
whilst humming tunes from a centuries lost pride.
Hosting the lightness to awaken this soul,
then fooling the seasons into the swelling of tides.

Drawing the heat from the earths centre crust,
then pulling myself across vast lands of lust.

Peeling from shadows reflections so bright,
that masked my life in peril and fight.

Its patterns so grand, formed in beauty by hand,
beyond imagination, paradise and creation.
But then it's back to the dust, my whole sense of being.
Just a witness bestowed upon man for his seeing.

Images and Dreams

I scooped out the sun to carve a curve, crazed moon
and tinselled the stars to create a backdrop, diadem.
I froze the sun until the icicles appeared
and decked a fir tree with ice crystals pearls

From the wind I created a faint gentle breeze
and enticed from the trees the falling of leaves.
From the land I dug out a long winding path
for autumns, spring and winters aftermath.

I collected the snow from an ice mountain cap
and watered the earth from my mother milked pap.
I stole a rainbow from heaven above,
cascading the colours to form a picture of love.

I took a drop of water from the ocean blue
and poured it into a lake, only for you.
I housed it with salmon, mallards and drakes
and awaited on its banks for you to awake.

I then built a house from an oak hollow tree
and dropped into it, a family for me.
It loved me with emeralds and roses deep blue
and kept me safe in its sincerity, so true.

The Tomb

I live in the depth of the darkest tomb,
the heaviest doom caved in from above.
It weighs, invades the vastness of space
and buries me blind without shadow or trace.

Engulfed by the pressure to extinguish my being,
I'm bound to a cross without anyone seeing.
I fall through the craters of heaven and earth,
then surrender to the sealing of a death open birth.

Remembering

I've forgotten all that's gone before,
Like space created from a wedged open door.
Unfolding time from present to past,
Threatening to catch up when I think I'm last.

Photos of characters and images portrayed,
a life not lived in truth, I pray.
An illusion of facade with all its ties,
that second in time that depicts a lie.
Stark and bold in memory it's clear,
that's not me, him or her.
The fresh young babe, there in arms,
is a multi tasker who works on farms.
And she's the wife of a millars tale
and has given birth to more than twelve.
As for me my shell has changed,
a full grown granny but not so strange,
with a wrinkle here, a wrinkle there
but a red hot goer, if I'm fair.

Awaiting questions of what comes first,
my being, birth or what's just emerged.
Relieved to find I'm not there but here,
and open to that of what I fear.
A falling out into this space,
the past, future, here and now,
in all it's grace.

My Lost Merry Maker

Pendulum pants, poco dot smiles and chequered tears,
jostling heart my motives bid.
Whirly whistles and curly toes,
dickey bowed shirt in a world of woe.
Bottled up and banned from show,
and kept from voice in cheer and song.

Oh sweet charm of dual in nature,
peeping through this crack of dawn.
Pennies thrown from my heart,
to move this characters life apart.

Oh welcomed guest from the corridor of mirrors,
Wondering mistral, jester, joker all in one.
Where did I loose you? Where have you gone?

Sequined hems, buckled beads and button holes.
The cherry nosed prince of life and soul.
Thick white lips with sadness, laughter hold.
With utmost pleas from a saddened heart,
I called upon your presence sweet,
'scrape the layers of mired mood and merge within this space of mine'.

Opposites

Oh awesome presence tender, sublime,
thunder the toll bell against lightened chimes.
Tower the pulpit, Gods true given grace.
Echoes of prayer in a feared sacred place.

From the tide of wrath
to ripples so soft.
Offerings of wealth, flesh, being and self.
Missionary, prophet, lay preacher and stealth.

Small is your great and all is your none,
a paradox of truth in your meaning for some.
Abolisher, creator the giver of time,
the darkness of light this lover of mine.

Second Birth

Captured by the beloved divine
and carried on eagle wings sublime.
Past, future and present, all bestowed.
My attachments, egos and all my woes.

Pulled through nature, it and me,
a folly tale of what I see.
Blinkered blocked imaginations.
Mistaken magnet of attractions.

My nakedness emerged into being,
without time, concept, place or feeling.
Then birthed into this sacred space,
my God to meet with, face to face.

Walking with Thee

I fell to my knees in the valley of Bacca, blind,
when flood like waters poured from my eyes.
As I gazed at the priests, saints and kings, I wept
out from my soul for their temples, so fine.

I wondered through paths of hot desert sands that
tore the skin from my face, feet and hands.
Then from your oasis I bathed my body to free the
pain burnt scars that I carried with me.

And as I passed through ageless hallways of time,
I marvelled upon your healings, forgiveness and love divine.
Then I drew myself from the murky silk muck to
reach the hem of your garment, so pure.

I was then peeled back to my seedling birth that
even my dreams and vision told truths.
Oh true maker of mankind open to them that they may find,
the transcendent gift of your truth that binds.
I drank from the cup my Saviours blood and then
turned my back upon all rituals that lied.
With my prostrated body laid to the floor I awaited

with others for the opening of doors,
I patiently waited for what was to be.
To find a treasured true promise,
to be ever with thee.

Finality

I dragged my body weary drained,
Its flesh like appearance so cruelly pained.
Eyelids folded like water soaked clothes,
sunk and mangled a shell like poise.

Surging struggle in a fight to survive,
my spirit forged and feigned in strife.
And when I looked I had disappeared,
to embrace the end of what I'd feared.

And Others

Lost Self

I served him here and served her there and bent to
whim of human kind until myself couldn't find.
Then I paid the ultimate price and found
that nothing ever would suffice.

I gave up self to others, you see, without
questions, plan or motives to be.
I had lost myself and what was free and
ensnared myself into a false faked me.

When I looked I had disappeared and all
that was left was what I feared.
An empty shell and shackled being, masked
through others for their seeing.

I called to the echo's of what weren't mine and
patiently awaited of what I'd find.
But in dismay they didn't reply and I found again myself denied.
I had lost the me and sacrificed I and had
earnestly tried from the nest to fly.
But then found hanging from my shoe, a noose.
My parents yearnings that wouldn't let loose.

Alice's Journey

Prisms fading and fallen from vision.
Myriads of colour thrown in for reflection.
Cradled by synergies beyond all understanding.

Flushing oceans of blue and grey, beginning
the ending with no sense of time.
A seedling birth and falling off, drift wood
passing from a channel of love.
Tears swept down to cliffs shadowed green,
beyond the sunrise sinking to sea.
Plunging down to the seabed rich, wading
through fossils of abandoned myth.

Then, here stands Alice a grain of sand,
and all of what's left.
Resembling a monument of life after death.
Moving in a way like never before,
the opening up through a cellar door.

The Dancer

And there again the image appears that haunts me into being.
It lurks without and clings within unknown to anyone seeing.

Mingled bleakness, void the veil against
stalking shadows gripped in silence.
Tempting fate of an untold tale, a world of suffering penitence.

Its presence hangs the dimness grey that holds me in existence.
The blackness beds me in its claws, drags
and drains me with persistence.

Scooping the hollow of bowel holds, the loss of fight to then let go.
But bitter taste the time that grows, the
performance of yet another show.

To Francis

A travelling journey upon this bus, no option, choice, just a must.
At last to rest my aching feet, to sit me down upon this seat.
But sinking into blissful wonder a wetness
draws up to make me ponder.
Thought upon thoughts of what this could be,
a residue of water or is it Wee?

When changing to a different seat,
a mob and crowd of people meet.
This space invaded, such a squeeze, so many people here to please.
Busy bodies, brooding mode, conversations over imposed.
A cough, a sneeze and spray of spittle wakes
me from my dreamed committal,
to reach a goal of destination and arrive in
one piece in contemplation.

A wink of an eye, a stare, a glare, smiles, groans and vilifying moans.
Push and shove, this woman dear, a shopping trolley in first gear.
Don't look now but she's fallen down and
dropped her brolley on my crown.
Apologetic burbles, an awkward blush,
then stamps upon my foot to crush.

In rage and anger but in politeness posed, tacit
gestures and actions chose.
To soothe a calm and troubled tear
but never to return to this journey of fear.

Ambersham Green

All above board in name and deed,
an outer shell of wit, of grace.
An ensemble of etiquette manner seen,
these solid women of Ambersham Green.

Empty vessels and curtains hung,
tea and scones and butter cake sponge.
Poised positions of heel court shoes,
to attract a poor wretch like Mrytle Blue.
To click and clack and banter on,
to all the deeds of charity clung.

Intellect quizzed and gossip gained.
A casual drop to name and fame.
To quiz and train poor Mrytle dear,
an editing of her character, appear.
To form a layer, a distance apart,
from the authentic nature of her very heart.

Acceptance

His drenched frail frame fell to the floor,
polluted by a sewer and wrenched from the
bile that clung to the womb.
Detached from the skin, vile and defiled,
where blue bled puss poisons the mind.

Pendulum swinging the soother of time.
Blended and detoxified in a rhyme.
Chosen the tones the texture of tears,
the scum of what's left from all that appears.

More than Me

From one to two, three and four and when I look there's even more.
A rippled presence of reverberation as I
form these characters in their framings.
A portrait of each and everyone, my world
without escape and end undone.
Arising to their wants and pleads to fill their over pressing needs.

Ever waving for attention and then
there's Louise not even mentioned.
Just pretend that she's not there whilst I
distract her pleas through the other pair.
George and Charlie in awaiting and taken up in formulating,
If patiently they await their turn, their
eager passion they're sure to burn.

So I put George in touch with Lucy, fifth who's
been in the shadows reading myths.
I pull her from an obsession of intent from
avoiding a meeting of what was meant.
Lucy now prepped in persuasion begins to
respond to Georges admiration.
Now the two are in conversation and relieved to think
that it's not a nation, I turn to Charlie's narrowed
views who is now alone, his ego bruised.

Now he's wondering off the track and I'm
petrified that he won't be back.
So I gather him up in loving arms and
encourage him in all his charms.

All three now in the background dropped a
sense of peace in mind has popped.
But when all the three have disappeared I'm
aware of a fourth who's just emerged.
There he is in all his frills Sam the musician but he's standing still.
No melody of spirit, no joy or fun, no note
from his instrument now struck dumb.
I occupy him from my heart and try to fill this missing part.
But lacking a personality of what it takes I
end up adopting a load of fakes.
So I turn to Louise in forgiveness and bid, 'please comfort
Sam who's lost and hid from friends, pals and
colleagues amid.'
Louise in compassion with a purpose felt, takes
up the part for his heart to melt.
She sings a song of love divine and breaks his heart as well as mine.

Now content the stage is free I look around and there's only me.
Just a break for an hour a day and peace at last from all their play.
But only to awake to loves due morning
to find six and seven in awaiting,
with tricks and tales ever baiting.

Foot note: Origen quotes,'vides, quo-mondo ille, qui pulatur unus esse, non est unus, sed tot in eo personae videntur ess, quot mores'.

Orphaned

Dribbled darling in a dress languished blue.
Depicting rose buds of smiles, green leaves in the hue.
Ginger whirls of ringlets dropped,
flushed cheering cheeks against a pale skin, mopped.
Oval dew your weeping eye and freckles fused with a blood red sky.
A feckless poise of innocence, a worried look so taught and tense.
This tiny tot of authentic truth, untainted, pure, beckoning her proof.
Coy and cradled in a world so cold.
No poppies of love from her heart to enfold.
Her arms stretched forth and then flung open.
This abandoned child, hand picked and chosen.

Sold for a Song

Christchurch Cathedral

Captured in a house of holy time,
with wings clipped and soul divine.
A candle lit for just impression,
a falsifying of all it's being.

Holy mother to bear my soul,
ripped me down so bare and shamed,
to scar my tissue, wound repeat.

Sacred soul of belief,
come to honour in its grief.
Pilgrim light, on horse back rides
hold to your soul and pass it by.

Temple bright and staunch it stands,
on backs of men, built precise,
to criminalize with state alike.

Persecution, pain, oppression.
This fine institute of collision.

Bound

Oh woe to this suffering, silent world,
captured to a deaf drowned land.
Laden, heavy dread the dawning, from its
fetter of history to ashes fallen.

Oh brutal gauntlet glove like holding
unleash your fist so cruelly clenched.
Release the sap from this yawning to
freedom wings that fly with feeling.

The damage done,
there's no returning.
Banished to oceans oppressed.
Lament the melody, sounds of singing,
Choirs and corals, muffled sinking.

Hells Henchmen

You pulled from the chords my melodic soul,

Then for seven years your electric
vibrations condensed me to dumb

till.......

my teeth fell
from their sockets.

From a Sonnet to a Shepherd

The gentle shepherds story told,
to keep the sheep within the fold.
Pronged with metal force his staff,
to keep this lamb upon its path.

To pitch, to fence and defend from fire,
the reign of protection with barded wire.
Tempered by his grace abound,
to electrocute this lost one found.

Never to run away again,
this lamb surrendered to its pain,
and in pretence complies with all,
abides its time before the fall.

This shepherd with his staff so still,
on guard for fear of gangsters stalk, where
foxes, thieves but Gods do walk.
Tender mercies and grace bestowed,
upon this lamb did God but show.

The shepherds fears of self alone,
abandons faith with all its tones.
Then released this lamb from its fate,
to a God possessed with loving bait.

Micro Chipped Sally (TI)

Imprinted thoughts, deeds and words,
moods distorted and memory not hers.
Puppeted from a keyboard afar.
Targeted, maimed, bullied and barred.
Random nudges, punishments, pleas,
beckons control to touch this key to watch
her intently bow the knee.

Top secret network, corrupted frauds.
Fiendish and reckless on life's intent.
Poor Sally's life now upside down,
a valued scapegoat, experiment.

Radar, electro magnetic storm, sold to the Navy for a song,
Encrypted language coded signs, copied to computer on line.
Shredded, printed paper paced,
completed job before the race.

Oh matrix misery where is she, what is she, and what is me?
Poor Sally circuited by more than three.
Now Sally's teeth are wired up,
the purpose for transmitting.
Receiving constant texts and messages and tuned to radio one.

Poor Sally's drained and weary self
tortured by this overload.
Fragmented, puzzled pieces fell,
frayed and punctured all her cells.

Now, broken down in disrepair.
Springs, bolts nuts and all,
lost forever in this matrix hall.

Pick her up to save her soul as Sally's fallen in abyss,
To meet with flesh and spirit kind,
to escape her stressed and frazzled mind.

Unaccomplished mission plans aborted,
mechanical men undone.
Found out in all its secret action,
with singing left unsung.

Devils, witches brew and wizards fight for
scrapes of flesh, what's left,
then bids poor Sally to a quest.
'Bow your knee to save your soul.
Surrender all or face the fall'.
Sally in an unknown place her maker to meet with face to face.
Her spirit in a desperate ploy un-expectantly calls out, 'Oh Lord'!

Torn in fragments to a shred, she lets go all the pieces.
She plants the seeds now overdue in earths
foundation love imbued.
Then surrenders up to one true God,
in a faith that she might grow.

Emancipated

Come holy reverence bishop, king and queen who
testify to save the people from themselves.
Lay your penance before the Lord and stop
this rod of love and punishment.

Bow not to man, power or beast to satisfy this carnal appetite.
Don't fear the world for its own existence.
Taste the punishment of the peoples experience.
Risk everything portrayed in the true holy word.
Stand up for love, mercy and all, and question
this barbaric torture of stately rule.

Release these people to themselves.
Give them all the true peace that you possess and help
carry for them this hell on earth in which they live.

Men born of air, forgotten of water have
mercy upon these chosen few.
Bow the knee in heavenly splendour in the
presence of this true holy one.

True God embraces offering,
True father gifts true will,
True living holy spirit births freedom, grace
and heals the people from their haste.

Escape

It forbade the flesh to sing its song
and plucked each feather from its wings,
revealing the wounded layers deep,
far reaching beyond existent time.

The jailers grip of freedom kept,
this poor sods bones bruised and snared.
His power of fortune kingdom wept,
a breath away from what they shared.

The victim pawned, the prize of suffering,
fragmented, frozen, tare and torn.
Split and spurned by its holding,
a sacrament of holy, ghostly being.

Peering through wrought iron gates,
an illusion of promise, facade and fate.
To escape this body in ascending,
a flight to freedom without ending.

Guardian angels, futile prayers,
cast eyes upon this malignant trial.
Then from the lesions, septic wounding,
the releasing of a butterfly.

Betrayal

Fiend and filthy accusers, distained in heart.
Search the web your own murders mire.
To stalk this weakened sadden wretch and quash
the attempts of the surrendered just.
You heartless mob of moral makers who waltz the waltz in
ballroom gowns, to loves non existent music
played.

You concrete, callous sufferings, deprived,
depraved in clandestine ploys.
Your mechanical Gods that crush the bones and suck on blood.

Loose the ties of bondage power fed.
Suckling mother of discontent measured against vampires militant.
Intrinsic in your nature divine to see your
prey quashed and flesh maligned.
As you batter and bend the corpse to bleed to
tear the essence from the soul.

Banal creatures in fine coats, satin shirts and boots of hide.
Pied pipers of ruttish, rule and reign.
Tips of tongue like poison polluted prey to
save yourselves from plight and pain.

You petty thieves of politic hold wrapped
around your licensed ways.
Bounded bled to slaughter led,
to tempt this sad and misfortunate soul.
And then took up your audience to view contrived, the evidence.
Pious pennies from towers thrown to sweep
and clean your conscious bowels content.
Nepotist nobles, belligerent.

No One There

A sadness crept into a setting before dawn,
to reveal a tale of a friendship torn.
My broken spirit in pieces lay,
the violation of trust betrayed.

In a desperate time of trial and need,
I begged a prayer on which to feed.
But when I searched beyond my plea,
a distance fell between you and me.

You were drawn to the street to evangelise
to warm a callous, cold love inside.
The angel driven to convert
an appearance of faith, that perverts.
To reach out to the chosen few
but then to turn your back to choose.
A Christ like image you care and lend,
then limit your share to a loving friend.

No room to be found in the Inn.
Slain and pierced and fallen to sin.
He bore upon his body scars,
this suffering rejection, maimed and marred.

The son of man with no place to rest,
His weary body put to the test.
Yet with love he holds my soul to bear,
when in the flesh there's no one there.

Revelation

This pillaging reptile in all its pride,
within walls of temples did abide.
Preaching to a audience,
faked love and charm of penitence.

Encroaching upon the backs of men,
magnetism that entices to a loins den.
Armed and captured within its scales,
a fearful learning from the bed of hell.

This vicious creatures vociferous woes,
to bid mans life from death below.
The barbarous nature of its needs,
of status, wealth and lusts impede.

Moves quickly, silently across the floor,
from head to foot its hefty core.
This slime green body draped to tail,
in convolutions that never fail.

The noise some pestilence prowls and preys,
disguised in brutal human affray.

Blasphemous faith of the holy word, a mask of
lightening from a humming bird,
crippled the innocence of those that heard.

A formidable power bedded in suspicion,
no fear or truth of contrition.
Purporting a truth through the art of man,
Michelangelo's God in creation of Adam.

This mindless form enraged, entranced,
lavishes its envy through song and dance.
Converting bodies for incineration,
soul and flesh for penetration.
To reap the land of what it's worth,
a trail of destruction, its living birth.

Siren City

Despairing powers in frustration turned
on the sirens in desperation.
She's off again and running hard poor Sally ousted out and barred.

Wells cathedral, church and foe on the run and lying low,
To catch a spy, convert a sinner and guarantee this royal winner.

A tug of war, surrender and plea to control this raging mighty sea.
Wasted toil in command and rank it's petty peril of doings, stank.

Rusty repeats of task and dance, ritualized actions in a trance.
Echoing from the depths of mind a masturbation for the blind.

Make haste my pearl, my cherished child and
run the race in how it's styled.
Lift your spirit to a God above and draw
from the worship born from love.

Grace and Heeding

Your foolish game and ploys revealed,
to love with a hand, to hold with another
and checkmate into position.
To set this God against itself and still preach good news in mission.

From bishop check king, to queen then pawn,
my knight in all his glory,
cut this chord so tightly bound into a new world freely found.
Between slavered wealth and all its health,
to release these creatures from themselves.

Heavens nature will prevail.
Freedom gates will tell its tale.
To pave a path not yet met,
to strip away facade and set.
Black on white and white on black,
chequered board in pieces.

To vanquish all its perilous moves,
all these pointless actions prove.
Rip these powers to a shed,
and unfold their senseless plots of death.

Masquerading Gods

Follow me tumble, follow me weed.
Follow its prey till morning dew,
to plunder and purge its victim bruise.
Pluck a chord to see it appear,
this invisible, silent enemy emerge.
Electrical surges and nights endured,
radar communicated from a heaven adored.

Tuned to a signal unaware, that rips to pieces and
to tear to strip this sod until he's bear.

Neither God, or Son nor Holy Ghost,
just a man made master with puppets beneath.
Pull a string and watch it squirm,
strengthen the surge and watch it burn.
Pursue the goal to strike it dumb,
to claw the catch until it's numb.

This travelling demon in all its robes,
to capture its prisoner and oppress its foe.
Parading within these holy walls
reaping riches for its own.

Robin Hood in all his glory,
tainted by the evil one.

Listen to their silent banters,
mingling within the heavenly host
Watch the sheep when they scatter,
to burn a scapegoat to preserve the most.

Make your haste and run from view,
bury your head under hedge and roe.
Dig yourself deep beneath the earth,
if you intend to hold your worth.

Suppression

Segmented words, thoughts disturbing.
Sharp incisions from memory searing.
Birthing sorrow and pain of existence.
What meaning and purpose, so heavy and holding.

Distinct pieces, fragmented, distain.
Lost, forgotten, emerging and mocking.
Thrust in a coop shattered and shelved.
Halting the movement of rhythms potential.

Buried and suffering in this fragile frame.

The Scream

Petty powers and relentless ploys.
Trumpton town police and firemen, boys.
Silent cities, church councils green.
Corrupt and cosy, costing creamed.

Penetrated echoes of abyss,
carved into the terror tissue of mind,
like a skewer tool in dragging cork.
Tortured screams of mildew blind,
the reaching to my socket eye.

Pierced pained colour of asunder,
lightening flashed, dubbed in blue.
Pinned to ground and air asunder,
frozen and hung to a high pitch cry.

Begging boulders to release,
beckoning to a grave, buried alive.

Separation, Loss & Yearning

Farewells

Autumn calls, the leaves descend,
destined and resting on their journeys, lend.
Rushing, rustling, shimmering sounds, faint light
droppings through forests abound.
Like soap filled foam in its falling, bubbling,
bending their meandering unending.
Then from a frozen breeze in season, bends crippled
and brittle to a yearly treason.
Tumbling trails, twisting and twirling, taunted and
tossed in lifes games loss.
Red flashing pink, green golden blends,
paves the way to their own winters grave.

Goodbye

She turned her head towards her mothers breast,
broken to pieces, her heart in her hand.
Watching the clock tick its way through time.
Extended minuets into periods prolonged,
will it be today or tomorrow already gone by?
Will I be there when she eventually lets go?
Memories of her hand as a child she held.
Images snatched from the windows of mind,
collecting the love of ages past by.

And now......
Pulled from the breast as the tears dropped down.

Just to be with her where she is.
Guarding her from this painful death.
A loved pierced parting of all that she knew.
Could I take her place in this time passed through,
laying the reefs to a kingdom of freedom born?
Securing for her a safe journey to be.

I touched her cheek as she slept there, sweet.
My spirit calling to her from a place deep within.

'Mother, do you know I am here watching.....waiting?
Cushioning the blows on your frail physical form.
Soothing your frame from the sonnets of my heart.
Dreaming your dreams to save you from falling.
Embracing promises forgotten and fading.
Our souls enfolding this moment of meeting.'

'My sweet child I'm here, let go.
Allow me to wander the skies alone,
to touch the heavens of where you can't go.
Remember me well and release me this morning,
As this moon above is ever pulling.'

Love
Mum.

No Time to Say Goodbye

Don't be sad on my sudden parting,
I'm with you in all you do, touch and see.
Memories fly with me in the morning mist as I
dream the dreams of our hearts entwined.
Immersed in spiritual ecstasy embraced, I see you every day,
Gods precious given gift, a sought out
diamond of reflective colour.
Journeying on foot where saints have trod.
There are no words for my leaving so soon.

But I am in the breeze of the trees travelling times eternity,
alongside and so close, you barely notice.
I'm taking with me all you taught, a kernel
prepared for heavenly realms.
I can hear your voice in the distance calling but don't look back
have courage to take just on step forward.
Soothe yourself with a love for life and live it in grace.
Don't give anything purpose or meaning just breathe
the breath of a moment un-imposed.
Be there in the present, forever where time has no demand.
And if you weep I will be there to catch the salt pained
tears and I will water the earth with love you've
had for its birth.

I will sow your seed upon clouds passing over that even
the rain will burst forth in song.
Blessed one from beyond
Our meeting just for a moment.
A flight through seasons upon an eagles wing.
So sweet the fragrance of your essence that now
passes by in the setting of the sky.

Grieving

I stood alone on the banks of the shore and
watched my spirit ride the silver crest waves.
Disparate parts of memory floating,
surfacing up from a deeper source.

Then I sank to my knees as the tide drew in to
tempt the image so crystal clear.
To hear your songs from beneath the waters, the
sensation of your presence near.

Enchanting whispers enticed your fragrance in
the gentle breeze of wind, sea and air.
Exhumed my every sense of being, this
vacuous empty space and yearning.

I trailed the turbulence of your past dreams dreamt
and fell into their stories yet untold.
Then I held you there in my awakening and
waltzed you through its perils, bold.

Then when the tide had turned its ebb I
discovered my shell like body bound.
Heavy in breath and soaked in sorrow for
a love I'd lost, in moments found.

Leaving

Sadness dawns then shines and arises upon new
beginnings as you leave this place.
Adopting ways of freeing and becoming.
Dancing and embracing with visions once formed.
Awakening to birthed permission of laughing, loving and crying.
Letting go yearnings of tomorrow, yesterdays and generations past.

As I leave you sitting, contemplating a feeling unveiled,
then opening to reflections of a moment in time.
Filling this space with breath like existence.
Entering into a landscape of now, whilst shapes
colour the shadows of expression pass by
and then here.........
A silence punctuating and pausing, the flow of
falling into this ever present being.

Loss

Phantom years of loss and rhyme,
lodged in memoir, dredged the deep.
Depth of ocean colour wide,
stained by scars the journey blind.

Putrid flesh and feast of time,
mirrored, mourned and made from mind.
Essence deep the spirit lead
to a sacred place of the holy three.

Loves Illusion

Love and Marriage

Poppy Pearls of Promise
Bequeathed to a poppy pink and petticoat ribbon frill,
my gartered lady embraced in mauve.
Rippled stocking leg laid bare, met with patent red the shoe.
Stained with lip stick tongue and cheek,
my tangerine angel of varnished blue.

A Buried Bayonet upon my Breast
Betrothed to a soldier in flannel grey,
his army regimented tainted blue.
Shields of armour hidden gold,
his blush fresh cheeks and pelican pose.
Auburn promises and shades of green,
black berries worn until death us due.

Merging

Eclipsed the colours of purple pale blues,
taped onto edges of sunsets bliss.
Overtures of love, faded of feeling.
Vibrations embraced in a single kiss.

Tantalising ambers enveloped in orange,
pampered creams caressed in beige.
Hidden compassion, shy and withholding.
A myriad of shades smudged into a cage.

Cradled streams in grey silt banks.
Pebbled dashed snow drops whitening the skies.
Yellow stained buds runs through emerald green fields,
Masking these moods of dismal fawn dawns.

Silver peach trees against iced caps mountains,
melting the blend of rainbows due.
Shaded shadows of love, in awaiting
showering streams of pink petals,
scented and falling.

My Secret Love

You touched the secret garden I'd grown,
from a fortified falling of blossoms thrown.
It awoke and purged my heart to call,
an urge of my feign and shy turning, pull.

It opened me up to a place not known,
the fallen layers I'd seldom shown.
The melting miracle of an ice stacked being,
a butterfly mauve, my spirit freeing.

You filled my thoughts, the day, the years,
an illusion filled with stained dry tears.
A tempting yearning to embrace,
tender soothe ripples caressed with lace.

Then came the imp to stalk and brawl,
to prepare me for a future fall.
The torture of a certainty unsure
a painful bliss of what's not secure.

So I turned my back on the future unknown,
to continue a dream of what I owned.
Then wading deep into the ocean blue,
I secured a hope that I'd found in you.

Passing Love

Lay me down sweet lover still,
twinned flesh embraced in part and whole.
Like dew upon the grass receive,
to sink to depths in sonnet posed.

Caress thy furrowed brow and cheek,
a pounding of your heart near mine.
Vibration of this pulse entwined,
this solid form to fill my mind.

Shag and tender, blistered, bruised,
to clutch thy thigh enraged.
Bear nipple crushed against thy breast,
erected moments in unrest.
Contours burning, passion of light, surge to
heights of mountains moved,
to crystal deep descending.

Sweet Refreshing

Do you hear my echoes calling?
Lover, tendered, embraced in dreams torn apart.
Lift your weary head.
Come bathe in the scented water of my love.
Hang up your troubled thoughts and follow me
down to the land that feeds.

Your dishevelled frame broken and barren,
standing alone battered and bruised.
Give up the folly of lifes intent to hold your self in senseless pride.
Abandon the wheel that forever turns to replace
the sketching of just another life.

Let me breathe into you the love of life,
refreshing moments in consciousness.
Listen and attend these sweet words given
and raise yourself from this lifeless prison.

Fade into my arms, ever holding,
your bliss and magic ever enchanting.
Rest and sleep your heavy eyes,
whilst I lament to you these lullabies.

Twinned Longing

My flesh awoke to your love newly found,
an unfolding affection of your presence, still near,
Tenderly holding my future, past, present,
releasing the wonder of my dreams ever dreamt.
Foretelling disasters before my foot having slipped,
hung on shadows of images turned grey.
Capturing seasons in full adulation,
and bereft in the urge of my yearnings for you.

Theatre of Dreams

Emerald blues, mauve marooned hues,
this ghostlike love of drifted dew.
Shades of shadows, the ides of time,
lay wasted roots upon fertile ground.

Smog lit pictures that tease the mind,
its blurring of illusion, the reality to find.
Pawns my heart to surrender its chase,
to fetid, fallen fields of grace.

A witness to their callous deed,
you watched them bruise my body to bleed.
A bitter taste, a corrupted truce,
this predators actions of abuse.

My lover bowed down and bound alive,
blinkered, buckled by an entourage of lies.
Unfasten the fetters, release and free,
this loge existence, to what might be.

Natures Naked Beauty

Time

The tides of times, a seasons unrest,
like a suckling child pulled from the breast.
Overgrown paths that once did wind,
eroded rock by the waters that grind.

The exist of guests from a gathering so fine, when
dawn falls to dusk, the sun sunk to moon and
stars in the sky.

The invisible seed the birth of its death,
A grounding of essence of all that is left.
Then wishing it was, that never has been,
the passing by of a kernel unseen.

Teacher

Embrace my spirit to unfold,
the teachings of your ways made bold
and plant a seed of what might be,
from the depth of the sea,
to heights of heavens set free.

The Rock

This cornered stone carved into the landscape deep,
that blunted the suns rays and splintered the bouldering tidal waves.

Changes

I carried the weight of the clouds dropped down and
caught the fragments flying from shooting stars.
I ran with winds from the Autumn nights and
drank from the oceans of raging tides.

I sunk to depths of the suns setting West and
danced with the moons overhanging the skies.
I sang with the dunes of whistling sands and
met with the changing of seasons blind,
then,
proffered myself as to what I might find.

Joy

Watered by the blood of teardrops wept,
effervescent bubbling world in ascending.
Sky above blue, reflection unending,
Vomit, flood of joyous elation,
Plundered and stunned by reality its flow.
Abyss with heaven in duality exists.

Centre Ground

Beckoned to the woods of natured time,
its breathing draws me, breath entwined.
Enveloped in its beauty holds,
my heart to soul, a mould in gold.

The trunk of tree, a carved inscription,
an arrow, heart, encrypted, 'Harry loves Kristin'.
Its out stretched roots plunged deep to ground,
a refuge home for each creature found.

Branches swooped high to sky,
for resting wings of birds, pass by.
Drooped the leaves in morning dew,
to moisten and feed its bark anew.

Random leaves cascade and fall,
breaks the moments of stillness stall.
Tumbling down in the air amiss,
a meeting with mothers nature bliss.

Thirsting

Fairest green blade of grass,
falling down to the streams ever flowing,
caressed, embraced in uniting the breath of life, nature entwining.

Sea Home

Born under the moon a thousand years ago,
gravitated to earth sunken feet from below.
Submerged to a world of foreign terrain,
Rooted rhizome, a melodic refrain.

Dredged the dark, thick, green, deep bed,
my body swamped, grounded and fed.
Shifting the tides, current and swirls,
tossing my limbs like a string of pearls.
Rafters of surf, white bubbled foam,
emerges and fades with no destined home.
Wave upon wave the rhythm of life,
birthing and breathing its depth without strife.

Willow Willowing

I found you in the forest thick,
standing tall amongst one and all.
How grand the descending of your branches fall.

Sweet willow leaves, tender pale,
cascading down, rippled green.

Oh Willow tree weep for me.
Bend your bows to touch my toes.
Wail your droplets of dew so wet.
Reach and take and hold me close.

Ground me with your roots, run deep,
to share our troubles, soothe.

Untouched

From a secret garden blighted fell
a numinous celestial being, tale.
Innocence bathed in pale blue arms.
Pink tenderness swamped in scented balm.

No Place

Rhapsody

Top hat tails.
Bucket and pale,
paradise pollen from a treasure trail.
Jostling jokers folly fallen
tears swept drenched, expressed and softened.

Peach petal blues, melodious singing,
penguins poised their proffered bleating.
Paper tissue shocked in colour,
puppets, clowns and scenes pictorial.

Plumage feather, favoured fillings,
stuffed and shoved in empty casings.
Allures alive a world in strife,
figures harnessed in dreamlike, rife.

Jericho

In your eyes of emerald green,
I beheld the knowledge of all you'd seen.
A world of destruction turned in on itself,
mans weeping, scoffers besieged by wealth.

Seeping lusts and secrets unfold,
folly and fake its image sold.
Scourged upon the temple stone,
the signatures of men engraved from bone.

And when they awoke from the dream of desire,
the walls fell down, foundation to spire.
Revealed in its place a spirit for all,
open, un-caged a temple without wall.

A corner stone alive, unseen,
a power of love that's never been.
From the seed of earth to heavens fusion.
a release of mans being from all pollution.

Running

Born from the belly of a whale, intermingling
colours and rapturous singing.
She and all her followers lost, to a cancerous
world fallen, at mans bitter cost.
Plunged into this radar state, her life mapped out before its fate.

Tin built graves muted and dubbed, bin liners,
polythene and energy that saves.
Inhaling rusted craters of stone, penetrating
force into skin, flesh and bone.

Clothed from the moss and earths mud healer,
she's pulled from the porous man made feeder.
To save her from an electrical state, from
a polluted, hidden, evil bait.

Escaping naked through the woods incline, she
feeds upon the forest, streams, foliage and pines.
A thorn thistle crown upon her head, ivy,
heather spindled rainbows thread.
Bathed and emerged deep within this ground, her life, soul, love
and happiness found.

Systems

Fragments fallen from a broken box,
The edges sharp and incisions cut deep.

A torturous stench of tragedies a loom,
Then a sweet pirouette of poison pierces.

Strange when the tides turn and seasons bid their wish.

The Caldron

Purged the pain drained from shame,
murderers, mockers, corporate corpses.
Penetrated purses, stolen flesh,
bodies varnished in corrugated mesh.

Limbs dropped down in heaviness weighed,
sight, sound, smell its suffering paid.
Numbness bliss from heaven's kiss,
paves the way to a mosaic twist.

Tarnished faith, devious charms,
infectious gifts, its mischief's farm.
Mansion, palaces, cankered deeds,
essence ripped from a flesh that pleads.

The Computerised End

Fallen pearls from the core of the fruit,
birthed, spurned from Gods stolen earth.
Climaxed creations from metal lined wombs,
the extinction of man to a worlds empty tomb.

www.ingramcontent.com/pod-product-compliance
Lightning Source LLC
Chambersburg PA
CBHW070631300426
44113CB00010B/1732